Stars and Constellations

By Gregory Vogt

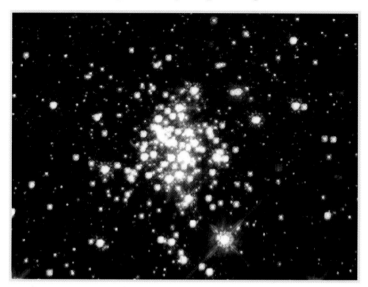

Raintree

OUR UNIVERSE

www.raintreepublishers.co.uk
Visit our website to find out more information about Raintree books.

To order:
 Phone 44 (0) 1865 888112
 Send a fax to 44 (0) 1865 314091
 Visit the Raintree Bookshop at www.raintreepublishers.co.uk to
browse our catalogue and order online.

First published in Great Britain by
Raintree Publishers, Halley Court, Jordan
Hill, Oxford OX2 8EJ, part of Harcourt
Education.
Raintree is a registered trademark of
Harcourt Education Ltd.

Design: Jo Hinton-Malivoire and Tinstar
Design (www.tinstar.co.uk), Jo Sapwell
(www.tipani.co.uk)
Illustrations: Art Construction
Picture Research: Maria Joannou
and Su Alexander
Production: Jonathan Smith

Originated by Dot Gradations Ltd
Printed and bound in Hong Kong and
China by South China Printing

ISBN 1 844 21423 0
07 06 05 04 03
10 9 8 7 6 5 4 3 2 1

**British Library Cataloguing in
Publication Data**
Vogt, Gregory
  1.Stars – Juvenile literature
  2.Constellations – Juvenile literature
  I.Title
  523.8

A full catalogue record for this book is
available from the British Library.

Acknowledgements
The publishers would like to thank the
following for permission to reproduce
photographs:
Cover Photo:
Don Figer (STScI) and NASA, title page,
14, 20, 32; NASA, 6; Solar &
Heliospheric Observatory (SOHO).
SOHO is a project of international
cooperation between ESA and NASA, 9,
10, 11; Hubble Heritage Team
(AURA/STScI/NASA), 16, 22, 35; C. R.
O'Dell (Rice University) and NASA, 18;
Roeland P. van der Marel (STScI), Frank
C. van den Bosch (University of
Washington), and NASA, 24; H. Bond
(STScI) and NASA, 26; L. Walter (State
University of New York at Stony Brook)
and NASA, 28; NASA, 36; Roger
Ressmeyer/Corbis, 38; A. Dupree (CfA),
NASA, ESA, 42.

Content consultant
David Jewitt
Professor of Astronomy
University of Hawaii Institute for
Astronomy.

Every effort has been made to contact
copyright holders of any material
reproduced in this book. Any omissions
will be rectified in subsequent printings
if notice is given to the publishers.

Contents

Any words appearing in the text in bold, **like this**, are explained in the glossary.

Diagram of a star

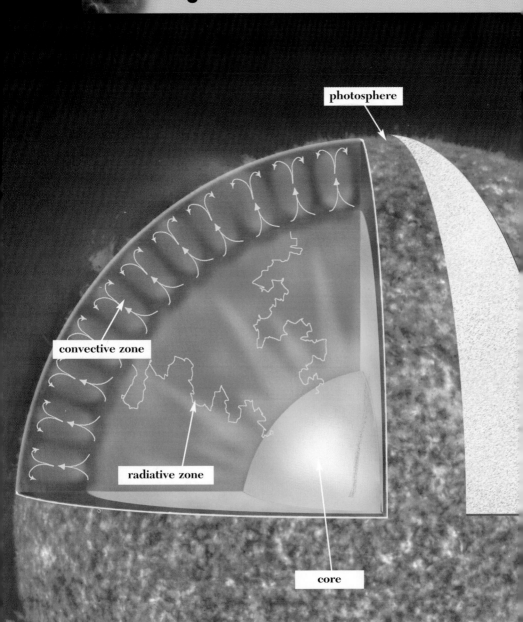

photosphere

convective zone

radiative zone

core

A quick look at stars

What are stars?
A star is a ball of very hot gas. Stars turn their **hydrogen** gas into **helium** and energy is released as heat and light.

Where do stars come from?
Stars are born and die in huge gas and dust clouds called **nebulas**.

What do stars look like?
Stars can be different colours and sizes. They can be white, yellow, red or blue. A star's colour depends on how hot it is. Huge stars are called giant stars. Small stars are called dwarf stars.

What are constellations?
A **constellation** is a group of stars that form a pattern in the sky when seen from the Earth.

How many constellations are there?
There are 88 constellations.

How do constellations get their names?
People named constellations after things the star patterns looked like, such as people or animals.

Light from thousands of stars shines on the Earth. This white stream of stars is called the Milky Way.

About stars

The black night sky is full of little white dots of light. These are stars. Stars are giant balls of hot gas that give off light and heat. The stars in the sky look small and dim because they are very far away from us. They would look huge and bright if they were closer to the Earth, like the Sun.

Astronomers believe there are billions of stars in our universe. Astronomers study stars to find out what gases they are made of. They try to learn how stars form and how stars die.

Stars are hard to see because they are so far away, so astronomers use telescopes to get a closer look at them. A telescope makes distant objects appear clearer and closer.

Parts of stars

Some stars are too far away for **astronomers** to study in depth. They must study stars close to the Earth to learn about them. The closest star to our planet is the Sun. Astronomers study the Sun to find out about the structure of stars. They have learned that the Sun and other stars are made up of layers of gases.

The centre of a star is the core. The core is the hottest part of a star. The **gravity** and **mass** from outer layers of gas creates pressure on the gas in the core. Gravity is a force that attracts objects to each other. Mass is the amount of **matter** an object contains. The pressure caused by gravity and mass crushes the gas at the core into a tight, heavy ball.

A layer of slightly cooler gases called the radiative zone surrounds the core. This is the thickest layer of a star. Energy from the core bounces around the radiative zone. It can take more than one million years for energy to travel through the radiative zone.

The convective layer is a thin layer around the radiative zone. This layer has large cells (groups) of moving gases. The cells boil upwards to the star's surface. These cells carry gases and energy to the surface of the star.

This picture shows gases in the Sun's atmosphere streaming into space.

The surface of a star is an active place. Hot gas bubbles rise to the star's surface. Explosions on the surface send fiery gas streams shooting into space. The surface also sends most of the star's light and heat into space.

An atmosphere surrounds the surface of a star. An atmosphere is a layer of gases that surrounds a large object in space. The atmosphere of the Sun and other stars can stretch out for millions of kilometres into space.

Atoms

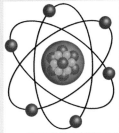

Atoms are the tiniest building blocks of matter. An atom is made of three kinds of particles, protons, neutrons and electrons. At an atom's centre is a nucleus. Protons and neutrons make up the nucleus. Electrons orbit around the nucleus.

 People need light and heat from the Sun to survive on the Earth.

Making starlight and heat

Stars are made mainly of **hydrogen** and **helium** gas. Temperatures in the core of a star are greater than at the star's surface. The outer layers of gas are very heavy. Their gravity pulls on the core, and the core's gravity pulls on the layers. The gravity and mass of the outer layers create pressure on the gas inside the core. This makes the gas thick and hot.

A special process begins when temperatures in a star's core reach 10 million°C (18 million°F). The heat and pressure of the outer gas layers squeeze hydrogen **atoms** together inside the core. The hydrogen atoms join together and make a new atom. The new atom is helium. This process is called **fusion**.

A star uses only some of its hydrogen to make helium. During fusion, leftover matter is changed into energy. The energy flows from the core to the surface of the star. The star's surface releases this energy into space as waves of light and heat.

Fusion is always happening in the core of a living star. It continues to happen in stars until they die.

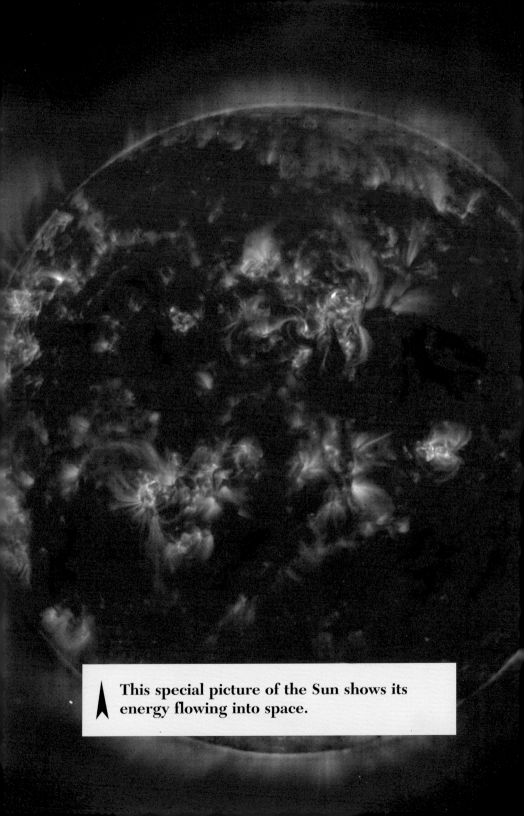

▲ **This special picture of the Sun shows its energy flowing into space.**

A long journey

The starlight astronomers see from the Earth is very old. After a star's core releases energy, the energy must travel through the radiative and convective zones (see page 8) to the surface of the star. The energy follows a slow path out through the radiative zone. The energy bounces and zigzags like a ball in a pinball machine. It may take over one million years before the energy finally reaches the star's surface.

Once at the surface, the energy flashes away from the star as light. Starlight travels outwards in all directions. It moves into space at a speed of 300,000 kilometres (186,000 miles) per second.

Rays of light spread apart as they move outwards from a star into space. The light is very bright when it is close to the star. The light dims as it gets further away from the star.

The Sun is millions of kilometres away from the Earth, but light travels so fast that sunlight released from the Sun's surface reaches the Earth in just eight minutes. Other stars are billions of kilometres away from the Earth. It takes millions of years for light from distant stars to travel through space and reach our planet.

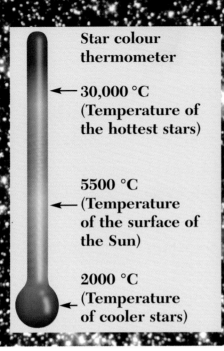

Star colour thermometer

30,000 °C
(Temperature of the hottest stars)

5500 °C
(Temperature of the surface of the Sun)

2000 °C
(Temperature of cooler stars)

▲ **Stars are different colours, depending on how hot they are.**

Star colour

Stars can be several colours. A star's colour depends on how hot it is. Very hot stars are blue. Blue stars reach temperatures of more than 30,000°C. Stars with medium temperatures are yellow or white. Cool stars are red. Red stars are less than 2000°C.

The Sun is a yellow star. The temperature at its surface is about 5500°C. It is about 80 times hotter than the hottest desert on the Earth.

Star brightness

Astronomers measure a star's brightness. A star's brightness can show astronomers how large and hot the star is. Brightness also helps astronomers tell how far the star is from the Earth. Dimmer stars are usually further away from our planet.

The size of a star affects its brightness. Stars can be different sizes. They can be small dwarfs, medium-sized stars or giant stars. Giant-sized stars give off more light than smaller stars. This makes them much brighter even than smaller, hotter stars.

Astronomers use two terms to describe a star's brightness. The 'apparent brightness' is how bright a star looks from the Earth. A distant, bright giant star may look dimmer than a smaller, faint star that is close to the Earth. A star's 'absolute brightness' measures how bright a star really is. The absolute brightness of a supergiant star would be greater than that of a small, dim star.

Star brightness is hard to measure. The brightness people see from the Earth depends on how far away a star is. It also depends on how hot the star is. The amount of dust between a star and the Earth can affect how bright it looks, too. The dust will block some of the star's light from reaching us.

Hundreds of stars are forming in this nebula in Galaxy NGC 4214.

Life cycle of a star

The space between stars, planets and other objects in outer space is not empty. It contains small amounts of gas and dust that people cannot see.

In some places, gravity pulls the dust and gas into clouds. The thick clouds of dust and gas are called **nebulas**. Stars are born in nebulas. They also die in nebulas.

The dust in nebulas is made up of tiny, solid particles. The particles are mainly made of **carbon** and **silicates**. They may also contain rocky materials. Dust grains may also be coated in ice.

Stars are made of gases that come from nebulas. **Hydrogen** is the main gas in nebulas. Nebulas may also contain **helium**, oxygen and **nitrogen** gases.

Protostars

Stars are not living creatures, but **astronomers** describe stars as having life cycles. A star's life cycle includes birth, life and death.

A star's life cycle begins inside a nebula. Many stars can be born inside one nebula. **Gravity** pulls some of the nebula's particles of gas and dust together. Thick clumps of gas and dust form. Each clump has a gravitational pull. This pulls the clumps towards each other. They begin to rotate and orbit.

Over millions of years, the clumps grow. The gas and dust in the centre of each clump get hotter and thicker. Some of the clumps are likely to become stars. These clumps are called protostars. A protostar is very hot, but does not give off starlight or heat.

Eventually, the temperature in the protostar gets hot enough to cause **fusion** in its centre. Fusion begins to turn hydrogen into helium and releases energy. The protostar is then a true star because it gives off the energy as light and heat.

This is a picture of the Great Orion nebula. Many protostars are forming inside this nebula.

Most of the stars in this star cluster are middle-aged or older.

Middle age

A middle-aged star is in the middle of its life cycle. It can stay the same for millions of years. Fusion takes place in its core continuously. The star makes helium and releases energy as heat and light.

The Sun is a middle-aged star. Scientists believe it has been turning hydrogen into helium and energy for about five billion years.

During fusion, the Sun burns up the gas it is made of. Every second, about 600 million metric tons of hydrogen change to helium in the Sun's core. This process turns 4.4 million metric tons of the hydrogen into energy. That means the Sun uses up 4.4 million metric tons of fuel every second.

However, there is no need to worry about the Sun running out of hydrogen gas. The Sun is very big. Scientists believe it will shine for at least another five billion years.

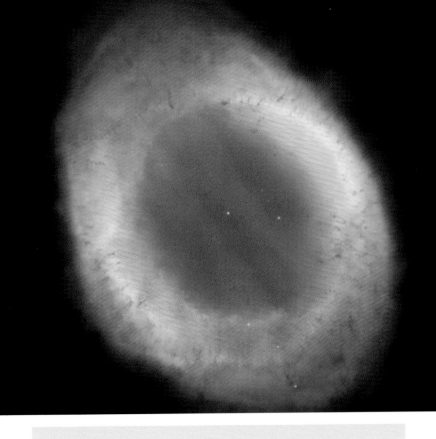

A dying star made the Ring nebula. The star shed several of its gas layers into space.

Death

Eventually, stars use up all their fuel and die. How long this takes depends on the star. Large, hot stars use up their fuel quickly. They are the brightest stars, but they last only about 10 million years. Smaller, cooler stars like the Sun use their fuel slowly. These stars last around 10 billion years.

Star fact

Star explosions make new elements, such as the metals iron and nickel. Explosions toss these **elements** out into space. In time, the elements become part of nebulas where new stars are born. Some of the leftover gas and dust from these exploding stars will form planets. Some scientists believe the Earth was formed from elements created by ancient star explosions.

Stars can die in two ways. Small, cool stars die slowly by shedding some of their gases. The outer gas layers shoot out into space. The stars become very bright and large as they shed their outer layers.

Only a small core of gases is left after the star's outer layers are gone. This core is called a white dwarf star. Over time, the white dwarf star cools and becomes a black dwarf star.

Large, hot stars die differently. They do not shed rings of gas gradually as they die. Instead, they explode all at once. The explosion destroys the entire star. While they are exploding, stars are called supernovas. Gas and dust from supernovas sometimes form new nebulas.

Black holes

Some scientists believe that massive supergiant stars form black holes when they die. A black hole is an object in space with such great gravity that nothing moves fast enough to escape from it, not even light.

Some supergiants cave in on themselves when they die. Their outer layers fall into the core instead of exploding into space. The star gets smaller and smaller until it seems to disappear. It has then become a black hole.

Even so, the black hole has not disappeared. It is really there, but no one can see it. It looks black because no light can leave the surface of a black hole. A black hole's gravity is too strong, and light cannot escape.

To understand this, imagine a person trying to jump off the Earth. A person would have to jump up at a speed of 40,000 kilometres per hour (25,000 miles per hour) to escape the Earth's gravity field and float into space. The Earth's gravity will pull a person's body back down if he or she jumps any slower.

The gravity of a black hole is much stronger than the Earth's gravity. Anything coming near a black hole is pulled in and crushed. Dust and gas falling in a black hole swirl around it like water going down a drain. The swirling gas forms a disc surrounding the black hole. The disc is called an accretion disc. Astronomers look for accretion discs to find black holes.

Powerful space telescopes are needed to see white dwarf stars (shown inside circles) as far away as these.

Types of star

Different types of star, have different masses, sizes and colours.

Very small stars are called dwarfs. They are usually old stars that are running out of fuel. The diameter of a dwarf star varies. Some have a diameter over 160,000 km (99,400 miles) long. Diameter is the distance across the centre of a circle or sphere.

Three main types of dwarf star are white, black and brown dwarfs. White dwarfs are made when Sun-like stars collapse. They are very hot. White dwarfs are very heavy for their size because their gases have been pressed into a very small space. On the Earth, a spoonful of a white dwarf would weigh as much as a car.

> **This neutron star is very hot and bright. It is only about 20 km (12 miles) across.**

Black dwarfs and brown dwarfs

After thousands of years, white dwarfs turn into black dwarfs. White dwarfs run out of **hydrogen** gas and cool off. When they cool, they stop giving off light. They are then called black dwarfs.

Brown dwarfs are another type of dwarf star. Brown dwarfs are not true stars. Their cores never get hot enough to start **fusion**. They never give off light.

Neutron stars

Strange things can happen to old stars. Stars 10 to 100 times more massive than the Sun can become neutron stars when they die.

Neutron stars are the smallest stars. They are only around 20 kilometres (12 miles) in diameter. Unlike other stars, neutron stars are dark. They give off energy as radio waves instead of visible light. A radio wave is a kind of energy wave that travels through space.

Neutron stars are made up mostly of neutrons. These tiny particles are part of the **nucleus** of an **atom**. Gravity makes the star shrink. It changes the atoms inside the star. The star's collapse pushes the **electrons** into the nuclei of the atoms. The **protons** and electrons join together to make more **neutrons**.

Neutron stars are very dense, or compact. Density is the amount of **matter** squeezed into a given space. Objects with greater density have a great deal of matter squeezed into a small space. Neutron stars are one million times denser than white dwarf stars. One teaspoon of a neutron star would weigh roughly 400 million metric tons on the Earth.

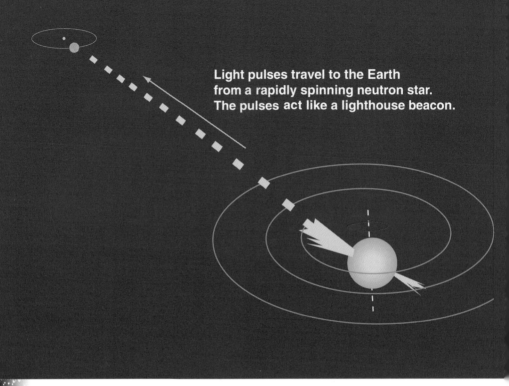

Light pulses travel to the Earth from a rapidly spinning neutron star. The pulses act like a lighthouse beacon.

This diagram shows how radio waves from pulsars travel to the Earth.

Pulsars

Pulsars are spinning neutron stars. They give off energy as radio waves instead of visible light.

All stars spin. Smaller stars spin faster than larger stars. Pulsars spin very fast because they are the smallest stars. Each time a pulsar spins, it releases a radio wave of energy that flows towards the Earth. The pulsar's spin makes its radio waves spiral outwards.

Astronomers use special radio telescopes that collect and focus radio waves. These telescopes feed radio signals into computers. The computers turn the signals into pictures.

Astronomers first discovered pulsars when they received their radio flashes. At first, some astronomers thought the radio signals were messages from creatures in space. Later, they learned that pulsars were sending the radio signals.

British astronomer Jocelyn Bell discovered the first pulsar in 1967. She discovered an object in space that released a radio wave every 1.33 seconds. This object was a pulsar. It was the first neutron star ever found.

Since 1967, astronomers have discovered hundreds of pulsars. Some pulsars spin several times in one second. Other pulsars spin hundreds of times per second.

Star giants

Some stars are giants. They average about one billion kilometres (600 million miles) in diameter. They are usually about 20 to 100 times bigger than the Sun. They are also about 10,000 times brighter than the Sun.

Some giant stars are red. The red colour means they are relatively cool. Red giant stars have a surface temperature of about 2700°C.

Other giant stars are blue. These giant stars are much hotter than red giants, but they are also smaller. Blue giants are up to 20 times larger than the Sun.

Blue giants are very bright. A blue giant is about 250,000 times brighter than the Sun. Rigel is one of the brightest blue giants. It is about 50,000 times brighter than the Sun.

This is a picture of the Pistol Star. It gives off more energy in six seconds than the Sun does in a year. Astronomers think it may be the most massive star ever known.

Star clusters

Many stars in the universe are in pairs. Other stars are part of larger groups of stars. The stars in these pairs and groups often circle around each other.

Usually one star in the pair or group is very bright. This is the star that is easy for people to see in the night sky. The other companion stars are dimmer. The light from the bright star blocks the light from the other stars. These dim stars are harder to see. Astronomers must look through telescopes to see these stars at all.

A binary star is a pair of stars. Sometimes the two stars are so close that it is hard for people to tell them apart. The stars appear to brighten and dim in telescopes as they circle around each other. This is because the dim star passes in front of the bright star as it orbits. As it does, it blocks some of the bright star's light for a while.

Bigger groups of stars are called clusters. Some clusters have several hundred stars. Other clusters have millions of stars. Stars in clusters are very close together. The Earth's night sky would look very different if the Sun were in a crowded star cluster. The sky would be bright and full of hundreds of thousands of stars.

M80 is one of the most tightly packed star clusters in our galaxy. It contains hundreds of thousands of stars.

Light years

Astronomers use a special measurement for huge distances between objects in space. The measurement is called a light year. This is the distance light travels in one Earth year. A light year equals about 9.6 trillion km (6 trillion miles). The nearest star to the Sun is Proxima Centauri. It is 40 trillion km (25 trillion miles) away. Light from Proxima Centauri takes 4.2 years to reach the Earth.

Galaxies

Galaxies are systems of stars, nebulas and planets held together by gravity. Our solar system is in the Milky Way galaxy. The universe is filled with millions of galaxies like the Milky Way.

The Milky Way is a spiral galaxy. Its centre is a nucleus. Some scientists believe there is a black hole in the nucleus. A nuclear bulge surrounds the nucleus. The bulge is a large cluster of tightly packed old stars. Surrounding the bulge is a flat disc with large spiral arms of stars. The Milky Way looks like a giant Catherine wheel.

Astronomers believe the Milky Way contains more than 100 billion stars. It is about 100,000 light years wide. The Sun is located in one of the Milky Way's spiral arms. The Sun is about halfway between the Milky Way's nucleus and the outer edge of the galaxy.

Most galaxies are found in clusters. The Milky Way is part of a small cluster called the Local Group. There are about 40 galaxies in this group.

 The spiral M100 galaxy contains more than 100 billion stars. It is one of the brightest galaxies in the Virgo Cluster of galaxies.

The Pleiades star cluster is one of the most famous in the sky. People can see it from the Earth without using telescopes. This cluster is also called the Seven Sisters.

Constellations

When people in ancient times watched the sky, they saw that the stars moved in set patterns. The stars rose in the east, moved across the sky, and set in the west. Night after night, the stars appeared in the same patterns in the sky.

People from several ancient civilizations made important discoveries about star movements. **Astronomers** from ancient Egypt, Sumeria, Arabia and Iraq tried to explain why some stars appeared to move. They found out that the stars were not actually moving. The turning Earth made the stars look like they were moving. The Earth spins from west to east. This makes the stars appear to move from east to west.

Scorpio

Sagittarius

Capricornus

Libra

Aquila

Aquarius

Virgo

Corona
Borealis

Hercules

Cygnus

Pisces

Pegasus

Bootes

Draco

Cepheus

WEST

EAST

Big
Dipper

Little
Dipper

Andromeda

Cassiopeia

Perseus

NORTH

▲ **This modern star map shows some of the major constellations.**

Star maps

Astronomers in ancient times drew star maps. This helped them remember where and when they would see the same stars in the night sky. The astronomers divided the sky into smaller parts. They put the stars into small groups called **constellations**.

Astronomers have mapped the constellations for thousands of years. Today, scientists divide the sky into 88 constellations.

40

Constellation names and shapes

Each constellation has its own name. Astronomers wrote the names on ancient star maps. They named constellations after what the groups of stars looked like. Constellations are named after dogs, fish, bears, people and birds. There are even make-believe creatures, including a dragon and a half-man, half-horse creature called a centaur.

Astronomers gave constellations Latin names. In the past, Latin was the language scientists used. The constellation *Canis Major* is Latin for 'big dog'. The constellation *Pisces* means 'fish'. The constellation Cancer means 'crab'. The constellation Orion is the name of a hunter in ancient stories. The constellation Taurus is a bull.

Astronomers made drawings to show how the stars of each constellation made a picture. For example, the constellation Leo forms a picture of a lion. The stars of Cygnus are inside a picture of a swan. The bull Taurus is right next to Orion in the sky. The picture of Taurus shows it charging Orion. The hunter Orion is pictured with a sword and bow to fight the bull.

This is what the constellation Orion looks like in the night sky.

Constellation stories

Ancient peoples told stories called myths to explain why the stars were in the sky. Many of their stories were about constellations. Each constellation has a myth about how it formed.

According to myth, the constellation Aries is a ram with a golden fleece. People told this story about Aries. One day, two children were in trouble. Aries ran to save them. The children jumped on his back. The ram carried the children to safety. Aries was rewarded for saving the children by being made into a constellation.

The constellation Pegasus looks like a winged horse. According to a Greek story, Pegasus carried a young hero named Perseus. While flying over the ocean, Perseus spotted a woman in trouble. A sea monster was about to eat her. Perseus saved the woman and then fell in love with her. Her name was Andromeda. Pegasus, Perseus and Andromeda were later placed in the sky as constellations.

Orion was a great hunter. One day, a scorpion stung him and killed him. The goddess Artemis, also a huntress, was so sad when he died that she made him into a constellation, eternally pursued by the constellation Scorpio, the scorpion.

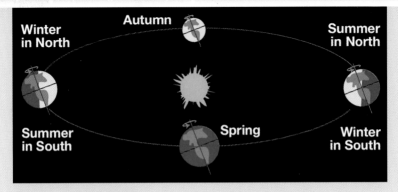

Winter in North · Autumn · Summer in North

Summer in South · Spring · Winter in South

North and south

The Earth is divided into two halves called hemispheres. The Northern Hemisphere and the Southern Hemisphere have opposite seasons. When the Northern Hemisphere is tilted towards the Sun, the Southern Hemisphere is tilted away from the Sun. This makes it summer in the north and winter in the south. When the Northern Hemisphere is tilted away from the Sun, the Southern Hemisphere points towards the Sun. It is then winter in the north and summer in the south.

Seasons and the Sun

Several things affect which constellations people can see at night. Observers can see different constellations depending on their location in the world. There are different constellations visible in the Northern Hemisphere and the Southern Hemisphere.

The Earth's movement around the Sun also affects the appearance of constellations in the sky.

The Earth takes 365 days to travel once around the Sun. For one part of the year, the Earth is on one side of the Sun. During another part of the year, it is on the other side.

Different constellations show in the sky during different seasons. In the Northern Hemisphere in summer, the Sun's light blocks out constellations like Orion. In winter, the Earth is on the other side of the Sun. People in the Northern Hemisphere can then see Orion, but the light from Scorpio is blocked.

Constellations helped ancient peoples tell what time of year it was. Each season, different constellations appear in the sky. Farmers watched for the constellations to appear in the sky. To the Egyptians, the appearance of the *Canis Major* constellation meant the River Nile would soon flood. When Virgo appeared in the sky, it was time to harvest the crops.

Today, people use calendars instead of stars to keep track of the seasons, but people could still use stars to track the seasons if they wanted to. Most of the constellations in our galaxy will stay like they are now for a very long time.

Glossary

astronomer scientist who studies objects in space

atom smallest part of an element

carbon element that is found in all living things

constellation (kon-steh-LAY-shuhn) group of stars that form a pattern in the sky

element substance made from only one type of atom

electron negatively-charged particle that orbits the nucleus of an atom

fusion process where two atoms combine into one

gravity force that attracts all objects to each other; the gravitational force exerted by an object depends on its mass

helium light gas, used to make balloons float and formed by nuclear fusion of hydrogen in the Sun

hydrogen lightest element in nature; hydrogen is an odourless gas

mass amount of matter an object contains

matter anything that takes up space and has weight

nebula huge cloud of gas and dust in space

neutron particle with no electrical charge found in the nucleus of an atom

nitrogen gas; four-fifths of the Earth's atmosphere is made of nitrogen

nucleus core of something; the plural of nucleus is nuclei

proton positively-charged particle in the centre of an atom

silicates (SILL-ih-kets) mixture of silicon (a mineral found in some types of rock), metals and oxygen

Further information

Websites

BBC Science
http://www.bbc.co.uk/science/space/
British National Space Centre
http://www.bnsc.gov.uk/
European Space Agency
http://sci.esa.int/
**Star Child: A Learning Centre for
Young Astronomers**
http://starchild.gsfc.nasa.gov/

Books

The Universe: Stars and Constellations, Raman Prinja
(Heinemann Library, 2002)
Our Universe: The Sun, Gregory Vogt
(Raintree Publishers, 2003)

Useful addresses

London Planetarium
Marylebone Road
London NW1 5LR

The Science Museum
Exhibition Road
London SW7 2DD

Index